CU00674150

The Teacher

A simple guide to daily life

The Teacher

A simple guide to daily life

Nick Fawcett

**kevin
mayhew**

kevin mayhew

First published in Great Britain in 2016 by Kevin Mayhew Ltd
Buxhall, Stowmarket, Suffolk IP14 3BW
Tel: +44 (0) 1449 737978 Fax: +44 (0) 1449 737834
E-mail: info@kevinmayhew.com

www.kevinmayhew.com

9 8 7 6 5 4 3 2 1 0

ISBN 978 1 84867 855 2
Catalogue No. 1501526

Cover design by Robert Mortonson
© Image used under licence from Shutterstock Inc.
Typeset by Angela Selfe

Printed and bound by CPI Group (UK) Ltd,
Croydon, CR0 4YY

ISBN 978-1-84867-855-2

To those of all faiths and none, who, like me,
seek a lamp to their path and a light to their way.

Words to educate you in wisdom, to help you understand insightful words, and learn how to behave wisely, uprightly, justly and with fairness. Words able to make the simple shrewd, to impart understanding and good sense to the young. Even those who consider themselves astute still need to listen and learn, and the perceptive to comprehend yet more; to acquire deeper understanding of proverbs and figures of speech, the teachings of the wise and their conundrums.

The Teacher[1]

---

1. For this and other words of the Teacher, see the References section, pp. 115ff.

Preface

This book is written with one purpose in mind: to offer words of guidance concerning daily life. It draws on words of ancient wisdom literature, particularly of the so-called Teacher in the book of Ecclesiastes and from the book of Proverbs – both largely ascribed to that renowned paradigm of wisdom, King Solomon.

This is not an overtly religious book, nor is its aim to entice you into some sort of religious commitment via the back door. Rather, it is intended simply to offer reflections on some key aspects of our everyday experience, in the hope that they may prove to be of help and inspiration.

The book is structured in the form of dialogues on such themes as hope, envy, fear and love, as though I am approaching the Teacher directly, seeking help and instruction. I have paraphrased the Teacher's responses – drawing these from the biblical text (referenced at the back of the book, to avoid breaking up the text) – and in each case have added further thoughts of my own. Not that I claim any special wisdom. Far from it: my insights are as fallible, as flawed, as inadequate and as culturally conditioned as the next person's. You may agree or disagree with my personal observations, but if they set you reflecting in turn then they will have done their job, for that is where deeper perception so often begins: in making time to pause and ponder.

I am no sage, presuming to hand out nuggets of wisdom. Rather I am a fellow-seeker with you, the reader, looking for deeper understanding but forever conscious of how little I have truly grasped. Yet that is the way it should be, for – to me at least – the chief lesson that the words of the Teacher repeatedly bring home is that, when it comes to the big questions of life, the truth, the whole truth and nothing but the truth will always elude us, genuine wisdom lying precisely in accepting the limitations of our understanding.

Nick Fawcett

About the author

Brought up in Southend-in- Sea, Essex, Nick Fawcett served as a Baptist minister for thirteen years, and as a chaplain with Toc H for three, before deciding to focus on writing and editing, which he continues with today, despite wrestling with myeloma, an incurable cancer of the blood. He lives in Wellington, Somerset, with his wife, Deborah, and – when they are home from university – his two children, Samuel and Kate. Delighting in the beauty of the West Country, Nick and Deborah love nothing more than walking stretches of the South West coast path at weekends, and Nick – as well as finding time for online games of chess and Scrabble alongside his many editing commitments – finds constant inspiration for his numerous books in the lanes and footpaths near his house. His aim, increasingly, is to write material free of religious jargon that reaches out to people of all faiths and none.

Contents

Introduction

I looked to the Teacher for guidance, for though I have thought long and hard about the business of life, I knew there was still so much to learn.

And the Teacher told me, 'I have focused my heart on seeking, pursuing and understanding wisdom, so that I might perceive the grand scheme of things.'

So I asked, 'Teach me more. Speak to me of the secret of happiness, of health and hope, love and laughter. Instruct me in the way of peace, patience, gentleness, generosity and life-giving relationships. And show me how to conquer anger, envy, pride and despair. Make me wise.'

Then the Teacher replied, 'If you cry out for insight, and raise your voice for understanding, if you seek for it as you would for silver, for hidden treasures, then you will acquire discernment and understand what it means.'

'I *do* seek,' I answered, 'and will keep on doing so. But, time after time, I realise that what I thought I had fully grasped I have misunderstood completely. Help me to learn more, to go deeper, for so much of life is a mystery.'

And the Teacher invited me to converse further . . .

Anger

A couple stood arguing close by, tempers rising on both sides. And as their anger grew fiercer so their words became harsher, delivered no longer to persuade or convince, but to wound and scar; to score points rather than articulate any points worth making.

Then the Teacher, with a sad shake of the head, said with a sigh, 'As surely as churning milk produces curds, and hitting the nose causes it to bleed, so stirring up anger leads to strife.'

'But surely we all get angry about some things,' I observed.

And the Teacher answered, 'Never lose your temper in a hurry, for anger dwells in the heart of the foolish. Whoever controls their anger displays great wisdom; a hot temper is the height of folly! Fiery tempers lead to arguments, whereas patience creates peace. A fool gives full rein to their anger, whereas the wise person is patient enough to let it cool down. If you have any sense, you will learn to control your anger.'

'But how do we do that?' I asked. 'How can we master anger, before it masters *us*?'

And the Teacher replied, 'A gentle answer soothes tempers, but an unkind word arouses anger. A gentle tongue is like a tree of life, whereas belligerent words crush the spirit.'

'So is anger never justified?' I asked. 'Is there nothing we should get worked up about?'

'God despises the following,' the Teacher answered, 'each being anathema to him: eyes that look down on others, a tongue that utters deceitful words, hands that shed innocent blood, a twisted and devious heart, feet that rush to pursue evil, a mouth that testifies falsely against others, and all who create conflict within a family.'

I pondered the Teacher's words, and I realised there *is* a place for anger – a need to rage against what demeans and destroys lives – but so often we misunderstand what that is. And I mused that were we to be even a fraction as angered by the evils and injustices of this world as we are about the most trivial matters concerning ourselves, what a difference we could make for the better.

But I saw also that anger is frequently foolish and petulant, more about piqued pride than right and wrong, about frustrated desire than justified indignation, about impatience than being truly aggrieved. For though we get angry when we are wronged, we grow angrier still when we are *wrong*. And what angers us in others is most often what angers us in ourselves.

And I recognised that when we get steamed up, we must learn to cool down, for words spoken thoughtlessly in the heat of the moment live on after temper subsides, wounding and festering beyond anything intended.

I understood also that anger begets anger, what starts out as a disagreement taking on a life of its own – insults traded, accusations made, grievances recalled; so fierce a blaze from so small a spark. Such anger not only hurts others; it also debases us, causing us to say what we do not mean, and mean what we do not say.

So then, what I have learnt is this: that when we say hello to anger, we say goodbye to sense, and what begins in temper ends in tears. The seeds of anger may be small, but the results cast a mighty shadow.

Anxiety

Then I said to the Teacher, 'Here is a puzzle. We enjoy lifestyles today that generations before us could scarcely have imagined, yet we seem to worry more than ever. Where are we going wrong?'

And the Teacher smiled and said, 'How special is the light of each new day. How wonderful to greet the sunrise. However long you live, celebrate every moment of your life.'

And I understood that if we would be free from worry we must live for the present, not brooding about what might be or what has been but celebrating the here and now. Yet, too often, our fears for tomorrow stop us from enjoying the delights of today, that which we fear *might* happen overshadowing what actually *does*.

I pressed the Teacher further though, protesting, 'Surely we must plan ahead, look to the future. Do we not have a responsibility to our loved ones as well as ourselves?'

The Teacher nodded and said, 'A wise person always keeps an eye open for possible problems and makes plans to deal with them – unlike fools, who can't be bothered and end up suffering the consequences. Never, though, brag about what you have planned for tomorrow, for who can say what a new day might bring?'

And I realised that though we must *plan* for tomorrow, we must never brood about it; that it is futile to dwell on what the future might bring, or on things we cannot change. For while our fears *may* come true, they just as well may not, and what is certain is that worrying about them will make no difference either way.

'But surely,' I persisted, 'we cannot help but worry sometimes, for catastrophe comes to all eventually, and to some more than others. Though it may not be helpful, is not worry natural?'

The Teacher nodded reflectively, but continued, 'A word of encouragement helps to cheer people up, but anxiety weighs down the human heart.'

And I saw that though worry may indeed be understandable, we must learn to let it go, for the only thing worry will change is *us* – for the worst. It won't stop our fears coming true, still less help us face them if they do. Rather, it will break our spirit, robbing us of the very strength we will need should crisis come. For, truly, it is not the things we worry about that hurt us the most but the act of worrying itself – our fear of fear.

And I recognised that the only way to conquer anxiety is to confront it; to stop running, stop looking over our shoulder, and face it head on. For when we let our fears do their worst, we expose them as foolish fantasies of the imagination and cause *them* to flee from *us*, rather than us from them.

My conclusion, then, is this: worry does not help us deal better with the future; merely makes us less able to cope with the present. Never ask, then, 'What *if*?' Celebrate rather what *is*. And let that be sufficient for the day.

Contentment

I watched the advertisements, promising bigger, better, faster, tastier – each urging us to want more, to be dissatisfied with our lot, insinuating that something is missing from our lives.

I saw the crowds bustling in the shopping centre, teeming in the supermarket, filling their baskets and trolleys in the mighty cathedrals of commerce.

I saw queues at the lottery counter and people hurrying into the betting shop.

I saw youngsters self-harming, addicts seeking their latest fix, friends popping tranquillisers and antidepressants.

And I marvelled that so many have so much yet feel they have so little; that most of us are full yet at the same time somehow empty.

So I asked the Teacher, 'Teach me the secret of contentment.'

And the Teacher answered, 'How happy are those with discernment, able to understand what really matters in life. Their rewards are worth more than silver, the finest gold or the most priceless of jewels – truly beyond comparison.'

'But wouldn't I be happier,' I suggested, 'if I had both discernment *and* riches? If I were wealthy then I would be truly content.'

Then the Teacher said, 'It is better to honour God and have just a little than to possess great treasure yet be in turmoil. Better to be poor and upright than rich and corrupt. And better to feed peaceably with your loved ones on dry crusts than to feast in a home racked by contention.'

'You tell me that riches are no guarantee of contentment,' I responded; 'that we need to rest as well as labour, and live at peace with family, friend, neighbour and self. What, then, should I seek above all?'

And the Teacher answered, 'I ask for two things only before I die; two things that I hope will not be refused me. To be saved, first, from being a liar and a cheat. And second, to be neither rich nor poor, but simply to have sufficient for my daily needs.'

Then I understood that a full heart is worth more than a full wallet, and a generous spirit more than a generous income. And I saw that nothing is to be more highly prized than a mind at peace with itself and others; a life at one with the world and the one behind it all.

And I recognised that contentment lies not outside us but within, not in what we might have but in what we have already: in living rather than striving.

I saw too that our frantic pursuit of contentment so often leads to nothing, our searching causing us instead to lose our way, our grasping to loosen our hold, our fretting to add to our disquiet. For we seek for trinkets among treasure, treading blossom beneath our feet as we pass unaware through a world rich in beauty.

Yet for the one with eyes to see, life already overflows, and for those with discernment each day already sings for joy.

The lesson, then, is this: instead of brooding about what you haven't got, give thanks for what you *have*, for when we have learnt to be content in all circumstances, then we will be content in any.

Criticism

I shared my thoughts with others, certain they would agree, but they shook their heads and questioned my reasoning. And they showed weaknesses in arguments I'd thought strong, bias in what I'd considered impartial, inconsistencies in what I'd believed held together.

Yet, far from learning from their insights, I was piqued, reluctant to listen further. So I dug in my heels and clung to my opinion, even though I knew it to be flawed.

Then I said to the Teacher, 'Speak to me of criticism, of what it may teach us if we have ears to hear.'

And the Teacher answered me, 'A wise criticism is like a gold ring or an ornament to those who are willing to listen.'

'How so?' I asked.

'Whoever takes note of good advice,' continued the Teacher, 'is on the path to life, but those who reject criticism go astray. Anyone who ignores wise counsel despises themselves, but whoever heeds reproof grows in understanding.'

'But criticism belittles people,' I protested. 'Should we not build each other up instead?'

'It is much better to be criticised honestly for your faults,' answered the Teacher, 'than to have someone, out of a misplaced sense of love, keep them from you.'

Then I realised that though criticism is not always well founded, it is always worth considering, for it can help us to see what we would otherwise fail to notice. For though we think we understand our weaknesses, most of us are our own worst critic in everything except that in which we should be. For what we cannot bear to countenance, we rarely dare to consider.

Yet that to which we close our ears is often what we most need to hear, and what is closest to the truth is what we push furthest from our thoughts. Better, though, to see our faults for what they are than mistake them for virtues. Better to get real than maintain an illusion. Praise may sharpen the ego, but criticism hones the character.

I saw also that before we criticise we must look first into our own heart, for the faults we condemn in others are too often those most deeply rooted in ourselves.

And I saw that if our words are to be more than empty carping or vindictive censure, they must be delivered gently and with love, never spoken with resentment or relish, but aiming to bless rather than curse, strengthen rather than undermine, add rather than subtract.

What I have learnt is this: the surest way to get above ourselves is to think we're above *criticism*. So then, before we reject what is painful to hear, better to *reflect* on it first, for though the truth may hurt, it may also heal. And though too much criticism may crush the spirit, too little will surely swell the head.

Deceit

'It wasn't me,' she said. 'Honestly!' And I believed her. But I was wrong to do so. For it *was* her, and she wasn't being honest at all.

Only I couldn't condemn her, for I'd done the same myself, too many times to mention: twisting the truth to suit my purposes, hiding it to save my blushes, denying it to escape censure or recrimination.

And I said to the Teacher, 'Speak to me of deceit.'

'Those whose path is honest,' the Teacher replied, 'have nothing to fear; those with something to hide will be exposed.'

And I saw that though lying may seem to our advantage, ultimately it is the road to ruin, for however much we may try to hide the truth, it finds us out, and though we strive to ignore it, it gnaws away within.

Better, then, to admit our mistakes than run from them; to come clean than be smeared with dirt later.

Then I said to the Teacher, 'Why, then, do we lie? Teach me about truth and falsehood and where they lead us.'

And the Teacher answered, 'A corrupt person earns an illusory profit; the one who sows honestly reaps a clear reward. What is gained dishonestly may taste sweet for a moment, but later it will seem as though your mouth is full of grit. A good name is preferable to wealth; respect to gold or silver. An honest answer is as special as a passionate kiss.'

I saw, then, that trust is easily broken but hard to restore, and that once we have proven false, few will believe us true. For if we dissemble in little, then why not in much? And if we deceive in small things, why not also in large?

I saw, too, that though some lies can be innocent enough, told to save from hurt or protect from awkwardness, most deception aims to hide the truth rather than shield people from it. What we cannot gain by right we gain by stealth. What we struggle to win by fair means we win instead by foul.

Yet when we deceive others we deceive also ourselves, and though the prize may be great the cost is greater, for deceit diminishes us as people and robs us of self-respect – the larger the falsehood the smaller we become. Better to enjoy a little honourably than to live a lie. Better to earn trust than dishonest gain, a good name than a poor reputation.

I saw also that deceitfulness damages not just *us* but others; that it undermines trust and destroys friendships, unfairly blames and falsely slanders, one falsehood leading to another.

My conclusion, therefore, is this: let your mouth speak truth and your lips desist from falsehood, for should you fail to earn trust in a little, you will fail to earn it at all. *Dishonesty* may seem to pay, but honesty pays better, for though it gain you the world, deceit will return as a thief in the night to rob you of your soul.

Despair

I talked to one in the grip of despair, not just low but utterly hopeless, such that they could find no peace, no joy, no reason to keep on living – each day seeming as pointless as the next.

And though I tried to comfort them, to show how much I cared, it appeared that nothing I could do or say could lift the clouds and restore their spirits.

So I said to the Teacher, 'Help me to understand what they are feeling. Give me some insight.'

And the Teacher answered, 'Everything is utterly futile, pointless, a waste of time. What do people gain from all the work at which they toil under the sun? A generation goes, and a generation comes, but the earth remains for ever. It is all tedious, more than words can begin to say. The eye finds no fulfilment in what it sees, nor the ear in what it hears. History goes on repeating itself: whatever we do is ultimately the same as what's been done before; there is nothing original under the sun. This business of life God has given us to be getting on with is not a happy one. Everything we do in this world is an empty illusion, a vain pursuit of the wind.'

And I glimpsed for a moment the pain of despair, the hopelessness of those caught in its maelstrom, sucked ever deeper into its crushing depths until nothing and no one seems to matter and life feels without purpose. I grasped something of the misery of each day seeming to be sapped of a little more joy, a little more hope.

'Is there nothing I can do?' I asked the Teacher. 'Nothing I can say?'

And the Teacher answered, 'Even the sweetest of songs is as vinegar poured on a wound to one who is heavy in heart; it is like stripping off their clothes on an icy day.'

I saw then that attempts to help can, rather, hinder; to lift up, instead beat down; to ease pain, increase it further – that what we intend as kindness can be cruellest of all, adding only to the burden of pain, guilt and sorrow.

For there are no easy answers, no magic words to spirit despair away. The sun still shines, but holds no warmth. The flowers blossom, but have no beauty. The birds sing, but their tune is bland. Though life is rich, yet it feels poor.

And I understood that what the despairing need is not advice but understanding, not to listen but to speak; to open up and be heard without judgement or condemnation, impatience or expectation, so that, however isolated they may feel, they will know they are not alone.

The lesson I have learnt is this: where lives lie broken and despair hangs heavy, never seek to give answers; give rather of yourself – your time, your love, your care – for where life has lost its spark, we can only gently fan the smouldering embers until the flame ignites once more. And should you be the one despairing, do not lose heart . . . for though you may not see it now, and may not think it possible, night will finally give way to morning, tears to laughter, and winter again to spring.

Drunkenness

I passed by a man staggering in the street, so drunk that he did not know who he was. I spotted youths brawling, singing, shouting outside the nightclub, all inhibitions forgotten. And I came across people urinating, vomiting, collapsing by the roadside, heedless of their dignity, heedless of everything.

Then I said to the Teacher, 'What are they thinking of? How can they let this be?'

And the Teacher replied, 'Wine makes a mockery of you, strong drink turns you into a troublemaker; whoever is seduced by it is stupid. Those who lack self-control end up like a besieged city that has had its walls breached.'

I understood then how alcohol flatters to deceive, promising much yet delivering little; how it makes fools of the wisest and weaklings of the strongest, assaulting the body and impairing the mind.

And I realised that when alcohol takes hold, what we see and what we think we see are not the same; that how we perceive ourselves and how others perceive us are altogether at odds.

Then I said to the Teacher, 'Why, then, do we not recognise this before we let it happen?'

And the Teacher answered, 'Look not on the wine when it is red, when it sparkles in the glass. It goes down smoothly enough, but it bites you like a serpent, like a poisonous adder. You will end up hallucinating, and your mind will play tricks on you. But you will say to yourself, "How long will it be before I wake up and can fix myself another drink?"'

I saw then that the road to ruin is more easily taken than we might imagine, and that the further we walk it, the less we see where we're going, until we no longer know or care.

What begins as pleasure ends in pain. What starts as choice leads to compulsion. What we think we can control instead controls us. For though a little will not hurt us, it easily becomes more than a little; and what is genuinely moderate, compared to what we *assume* to be so, may be distant strangers.

So then, my conclusion is this: think before you drink or it may be you who ends up drunk. And think *as* you drink, or you may not be able to think at all.

Envy

The child opened his present in wonder and delight, rejoicing at the gift – until a friend showed what she had received, and suddenly his joy was tarnished, his pleasure lessened, his thoughts no longer on what he'd received but on what he'd been denied.

The worker received a rise, and celebrated – until she learnt that others had received more, and suddenly her increase was no longer an extra but an insult, a slight rather than a bonus.

The couple moved into their new home, and life was good – until they passed the new estate down the road, and in a moment what they had formerly treasured they began to despise, and what had previously satisfied now stuck in their craw.

Then I asked the Teacher, 'Explain this to me.'

And the Teacher replied, 'All human effort and striving derive from people's envy of one another. All are empty, a futile chasing after the wind.'

And the words rang true, for I too have believed myself fortunate until I contemplated the plenty of a neighbour. And just as I can be jealous of them, I know others may be jealous of me – each of us part of an endless and futile cycle. For no matter how high we rise, how much we have, there will still always be someone seemingly with more.

I saw then that envy will not bring what we covet any nearer; merely make us less content with our lot, turning a garden into desert, a harvest into famine, bounty into barrenness.

And I understood that though we may seem to have little, we are not necessarily the poorer, for the one who apparently has everything may, in truth, have nothing, and the lot of those we envy may be less rosy than it seems.

Then I said to the Teacher, 'Show me, then, where envy leads.'

And the Teacher answered, 'A contented heart leads to health, but envy eats into one's very bones.'

And I saw the truth of that not just in myself but in the world around me; in people consumed by bitterness and resentment, and relationships broken through jealousy; in friends estranged, wealth and success having driven a wedge between them, trust overwhelmed by suspicion and camaraderie by enmity.

Then I understood the words of the Teacher: 'Wrath is forbidding, anger is overwhelming, but who is able to stand before envy?'

The lesson is this: envy may be understandable, but it is never advisable, for in the endless quest for gain lies the surest path to loss. Better to count your own blessings than those of a neighbour, for there will be no time left then to envy the good fortune of others. Brood not over what you wish you had; celebrate instead what you have today, and be thankful.

Flattery

I saw a fool feted for their wisdom, a journeyman hailed as a genius, a beginner likened to a master. And they exulted in the praise, preening themselves like portentous peacocks, convinced of their merit. And while they boasted, a multitude sniggered behind their back.

Then I said to the Teacher, 'Speak further on this. Tell me what it means.'

And the Teacher replied, 'Whoever flatters their neighbour is casting a net that their neighbour may well end up getting trapped in.'

Then I saw that what we want to hear and what we need to hear are altogether different, those who pander to our ego finding a receptive ear, yet those who challenge our cherished self-perceptions meeting instead with a closed mind. For we are all proficient at deceiving ourselves, never mind needing help to do so from another. And without someone to challenge us, we all struggle to accept unwelcome truths.

And I saw that flattery sets us up for humiliation, fostering illusions that need to be questioned and expectations that ought to be checked. Yet honesty is hard to find, for it costs little to give praise, and all like to receive it, whereas to bring down to earth is harder, welcomed by few and resented by most.

Then I said to the Teacher, 'Should I truly shatter someone's illusions? Can that ever be of help?'

And the Teacher answered, 'Whoever delivers a well-earned rebuke will ultimately be more appreciated than those who pander to our vanity.'

I realised then that though many welcome flattery, few will finally be thankful for it, and though honesty may bring pain for a moment, it will ultimately save from hurt. For the words of a flatterer may appear sweet, but the taste they leave is sour, whereas words of truth may be hard to swallow, but are good medicine, helping to make us whole.

Better to know what we *can* do than vainly attempt what we can't. Better to attain the moon than chase hopelessly after the stars.

My conclusion, then, is this: do not let praise go to your head, or you'll surely stumble and fall. Listen as much to those who question as to those who flatter, as much with your mind as with your heart, as much to what deflates as delights you, and you will not be led astray.

Forgiveness

I saw a family divided, brother from brother, mother from daughter, father from son – what had begun as a disagreement having turned to a feud: opinions hardened, positions entrenched. Words had been spoken, insults traded, and none could forgive.

Then I said to the Teacher, 'Speak to me of forgiveness, of making peace.'°

And the Teacher answered, 'Friendship prospers where people are willing to admit mistakes; nagging about them, instead, divides even the most steadfast of friends.'

Then I was ashamed, for though I seek to forgive, I fail to do so, and though I strive to let go, I keep hold instead, dredging up the same mistakes, resurrecting the same grievances, raising the same complaints. For it is easier to hold on to resentment, no matter what the price, than to let it go without recompense.

And I saw how a failure to forgive destroys relationships, denying the opportunity to move on; how the one wronged becomes the one who wrongs, the one hurt the one who hurts, the one refusing to forgive the one most in need of forgiving. For bitterness poisons not just others but ourselves most of all.

So I asked the Teacher, 'Show me the secret of forgiveness.'

And the Teacher replied, 'Wisdom nurtures patience, and teaches you the special gift of being able to forgive and forget.'

Then I understood that forgiveness must be learnt, like so much else in life; that it is an art we must cultivate rather than a gift we inherit.

And I saw that until we forgive, we cannot forget, and unless we forget we cannot forgive. For, like grit in the eye or a stone in the shoe, a hurt remembered constantly plagues us, refusing to be ignored. Yet if we cannot forgive, why should we expect forgiveness? And if the pardon we receive were to depend on the pardon we give, where then would any of us be?

I saw also that what is hardest to forgive is what we cannot forgive in ourselves; that what hits too close to home rankles and unsettles us, reminding us of what we'd rather forget, uncovering what we try to bury.

Truly, forgiveness breeds forgiveness, and resentment, resentment; a wrong allowed to fester is a wrong multiplied, while an error pardoned is an error resolved.

So then, my counsel is this: learn to forgive and to go on forgiving, not just for the sake of others but for yours also. And if you would truly move on and build a better future, first let go of the past.

Friendship

I thought him a friend, closer than any, and I believed the bond would last a lifetime – that however much distance might separate us and our courses diverge, still it would endure. But we drifted apart and the friendship died.

I thought *her* a friend, one in whom I could put my trust, but differences came between us and she cut off contact, all ties severed in a moment.

I thought him a *memory*, a name from the past, and never dreamt our paths would cross again, but when trouble came and friends had flown, he made time to write, to visit, to care – truly a friend in need.

And I said to the Teacher, 'Help me to know better who my friends are. How can I discern them?'

And the Teacher answered, 'Many claim to be faithful, but how many people are there in whom we can completely put our trust? A friend is a constantly loving companion. Some people are fair-weather friends, but a genuine friend stays closer to us than our own family.'

And I understood that true friendship is the rarest yet most precious of gifts – a jewel to be treasured, a diamond to be prized. For while many may *seem* to be friends, even counting themselves close, few will stand with us through the twists and turns of life, always there to turn to, faithful to the last.

Then I said to the Teacher, 'Speak more of what friendship actually means.'

And the Teacher replied, 'Well intended are the wounds inflicted by a friend, but effusive are the kisses of an enemy.'

I realised then that a true friend cares enough to risk our displeasure, even rejection; that while many will tell us what we *want* to hear, they alone will tell us what we *need* to hear, and in a way to which we can listen.

And I saw that such a friend brings sunshine to the heart and nourishment to the soul, for, should we question our worth, they remind us we are valued – that however ordinary we may feel, we are special in their eyes. Where we are ugly, still they see beauty; where we are weak, still they see strength; where we are broken, still they see wholeness.

So then, my conclusion is this: like a shower in the desert, a harbour in a storm, a flower in the wilderness, so is a true friend – a rare and precious gift.

Generosity

I saw a tramp by the roadside, and a busy throng walked on by, eyes averted, excuses silently made as they hurried past. But one stopped, offering not a token coin, but food, a blanket and a listening ear. And in that simple act of kindness a ray of sunshine broke into the darkness of the world.

Then I asked the Teacher, 'Help me to be generous in turn. Show me what I must do.'

And the Teacher answered, 'If you are able to help someone, never fail to do so. Don't tell your neighbour, "Go away, and come back tomorrow. Maybe I'll help you then."'

I saw then that what we think we possess can end up possessing us if we will not share it, and that what we cling to so tightly in fact holds us in its grip.

Better to be generous to a fault than see meanness as a virtue. Better to help others than help ourselves, for what we jealously guard swiftly loses its lustre, while that which we give sparkles more brightly every day.

And I said to the Teacher, 'Speak to me of goodness: of a kind heart and generous spirit.'

'Some people give freely,' the Teacher answered, 'yet seem to prosper, while others refuse to give what they should and somehow appear to be lacking.

A generous person will find enrichment, and the one who brings refreshment to others will be refreshed in turn. Kindness brings its own reward; likewise unkindness, its own punishment. The generous-hearted are richly blessed, for they share what they have with the poor. Those who make goodness and kindness their aim discover life itself.'

Then I understood that it is truly more blessed to give than to receive, for though receiving a gift brings happiness, offering a gift yields greater joy. To give pleasure is to share pleasure, and to give much is to receive more. Why limit to one what can so easily bless two?

I saw, also, that the generous give not because they must but because they may, not out of duty but out of joy, their heart as open as their hand.

And I saw that what costs us little can mean much, what seems small can be great, what appears trifling can be special beyond words. And the greatest gift is this: to give not just of our money or possessions, but of ourselves – our love, our soul, our being.

So then, don't just do what you *have* to do, or give what you can afford to give. Whenever you can, do more; offer that little bit extra; put yourself out for the sake of another. Learn to let go, to share from your paucity or your plenty, and you will discover riches indeed.

Gossip

'Can you keep a secret?' he asked. And his friend nodded. But the reality was different, and the juicy snippet of gossip was passed on . . . and on . . . ever more twisted and embellished with each retelling. Rumour fed rumour, scandal mounted upon scandal, invention built on invention, until none could see where truth started and falsehood ended. The one 'accused' had faced judge and jury, verdict passed, without even realising a trial had begun.

So I asked the Teacher, 'Why are we like this? What is it about gossip that attracts us so?'

And the Teacher answered, 'The words of a gossip are like tasty titbits; they soon make their way deep into a person. If you hear people running you down, don't take it to heart. For aren't you well aware, if you're honest, that you've frequently run people down yourself?'

I saw then how we feed on scandal, drooling inwardly over what we outwardly condemn; how, once we have tasted it, gossip becomes not just an occasional morsel but our staple diet. And the more we have of it, the more we want, and the less our greed is satisfied.

'But isn't that just the way of the world?' I asked. 'Does it really harm anyone apart from ourselves?'

Then the Teacher answered, 'A gossip divulges secrets; those who are trustworthy in spirit respect what's told in confidence. An insincere person stirs up discord, and those who whisper tittle-tattle break up even the closest of friendships. Scandalmongers will air in public what's revealed to them in private; so then, have nothing to do with them.'

And I understood that, for all our imagined virtue, we delight in doing others down in order to build ourselves up, in boosting our own esteem at the cost of another's.

I saw too how in exposing secrets, we conceal our own, and in highlighting errors we mask our faults, for in pointing the finger at others we deflect scrutiny from ourselves.

And I saw how the more we betray a confidence the easier it becomes, and the more attention it earns us the more we crave it again.

But I realised also that those who gossip *to* us will also gossip *about* us, their word being like a fraudster's promise, not to be trusted. And if we spread rumours about others, we will hear them of ourselves, for as we reap so shall we sow.

So then, my counsel is this: if you would hear no evil, speak no evil; and if you would have secrets kept, keep them first in turn. Gossip may slip down nicely – a tasty morsel indeed – but it will leave a bitter taste in the mouth, and life, of all.

Greed

I sat in the restaurant, and watched the diners feasting; in the fast-food store, and saw customers gorging; in the football ground, and spotted spectators snacking. And I saw bulging waistlines in the street, obese children in the playground, people so heavy they struggled to move.

And on that same day I saw pictures of famine and hunger, of multitudes so thin they were barely skin and bones.

Then I hung my head at the greed in which I shared, and said to the Teacher, 'Speak to me of a better way.'

The Teacher answered, 'If you eat honey, take only as much as is enough for you; for fear that, being full of it, you may not be able to keep it down. And remember, if it is a mistake to consume too much honey, it is a mistake equally to look for ever more praise and approbation.'

And I realised that, despite what some may say, we *can* have too much of a good thing, whatever it may be; that enough is truly enough, and to add more is to detract rather than enhance, spoil instead of improve. For what is sufficient leaves us content, while a surfeit leaves us bloated: the one a blessing, the other a curse.

So I said to the Teacher, 'Speak more on this. Where is it that we go wrong?'

And the Teacher answered, 'We labour day after day to feed our earthly appetites, while our soul goes hungry.'

Then I realised that greed takes many forms – not just for food but for so much else besides, our appetite for pleasure as insatiable as for sustenance, our craving for wealth as voracious as for any meal.

And I saw that greed is never satisfied; that though we have enough, we always want more. Yet when we have more than we need, we ultimately become less than we should be, for though greed may feed the body it starves the soul, and though it may feather our nest it leaves us ultimately empty. The more we consume, the more we are consumed, and the more we have, the less we appreciate it.

I saw too that greed is a form of robbery, for when we have too much, another has too little, and when we are full, another is empty. Our excess is their lack; our fullness, their famine.

My conclusion, then, is this: it is not only the stomach that can be greedy, nor just the body that pays the price; mind and soul can be left the poorer also. Like a ravening lion, greed lurks at your door, waiting to devour you. Beware!

Happiness

I saw a child giggling joyfully, a couple laughing as they shared a joke, a woman smiling gently at her partner, a man beaming in delight.

And my thoughts turned to happiness.

'Why do some always seem happy,' I asked, 'but others not?'

And the Teacher answered, 'Those who are miserable in attitude will be miserable in life, but the happy in spirit will feast continually.'

I saw then that happiness breeds happiness, and joy, joy; that to greet the world with a smile prompts the world to smile back.

'But how do we cultivate this happiness?' I asked. 'Whence does it come, and how do we attain it?'

And the Teacher answered, 'Happy are those who find wisdom and acquire understanding, for wisdom profits more than silver, and brings gain better even than gold. To those who grasp her she is a tree of life, and whoever embraces her will discover the secret of happiness.'

And I understood that true happiness lies not in what we *have* but in what we have *understood*; in discerning the beauty in the ugliness of life, the good in the evil, the special in the ordinary; in living each day, each moment, for what it is.

I saw also that happiness cannot be measured in terms of pounds and pence, prestige or possessions;

that it cannot be owned but is a gift held in trust, a feast to be savoured rather than a commodity to be stored. And I saw that if we attempt to hoard it, its beauty will fade like that of a meadow flower, here today and gone tomorrow. It is a fountain from which we must drink afresh each day, and if we seek instead to fill our bottle and carry it with us, it will bring sorrow rather than joy, pain rather than pleasure – the bitterness of loss and ache of nostalgia.

I saw too that true happiness comes not through keeping it to ourselves but through sharing it with others; that a joy shared is a joy multiplied, but a joy jealously guarded is a joy already tarnished.

The lesson I have learnt is this: if you would find happiness, seek it first in yourself, for if you discover it there you will know it everywhere. And truly, instead of *you* searching for *it*, *it* then will find *you*.

Health

I saw the signs at the hospital, pointing to different wards, different departments, and my thoughts turned to the patients and visitors: some troubled by no more than routine operations; others in turmoil, their lives turned upside down as they wrestled with diagnoses of life-changing illness, incurable disease.

And I was reminded afresh that health is a treasure we forget to prize until we start to lose it.

Then I said to the Teacher, 'Speak to me of illness and health, of how to cope with the one and maintain the other.'

And the Teacher answered, 'That which is pleasing to the eye brings joy to the heart, and good news restores health. A sunny disposition is an excellent medicine, but a miserable one shrivels the bones. The human spirit can cope with illness, but which of us can get by when our spirit is broken?'

Then I understood the importance of dwelling not on the bad in life but the good, not on our sorrows but our joys, not on our fears but our hopes. For though a cheerful heart can never guarantee we will stay well, it will help us to feel so, and though a positive spirit will not in itself conquer illness, it will make even the cruellest infirmity easier to bear.

I saw also that if, instead of dwelling on our own ills, we seek to give help and comfort to another, then our troubles will seem fewer and our burden less heavy. For to look beyond our pain is to ease it; to reach outside our fear, to lessen it; to forget our sickness, to disarm it.

And I realised that if we would know health in body we must seek it first within our soul, for should we be sick in spirit we will never truly be well. And though infirmities of the flesh are many, those of the soul are more and their power is greater.

I saw further that though illness may break the body and shatter the mind, the spirit will keep on fighting, keep on believing and keep on hoping, though all seems stacked against it. But I realised also that, strong though it is, even the hardiest soul can finally be broken, worn down by pain and sickness, fear and uncertainty. For as no plant can thrive if the root sickens, so no person can flourish if their spirit ails.

My conclusion, then, is this: celebrate your health while you have it, for like the flower of the field it is here today and gone tomorrow. And should health fail, then – however ill you may be, however diminished you may feel – stay strong in spirit, for you are still a whole person; not just a disease or condition, statistic or number, but an individual, deserving of dignity and respect . . . to the end.

Hope

I looked at the world and saw so much evil and sorrow, and so few signs of hope. What had seemed full of promise lay trodden in the dust, and there seemed no grounds to look forward; just the same old catalogue of woes destined endlessly to repeat themselves.

And I said to the Teacher, 'Is the future truly so bleak? Can we not hope for a better tomorrow?'

'You have a future,' answered the Teacher. 'Your hope will not prove to have been in vain.'

And my heart stirred at the prospect of new beginnings: a world released from its shackles, healed from its ills, cured of its madness, absolved from its folly. Yet as swiftly as hope rose, so it subsided, for had I not heard such promises before, only to see them broken?

'I want to believe,' I mused, 'for where would we be without hope? But so often it seems in vain. Speak more to me on this.'

And the Teacher answered, 'Hope unfulfilled makes the heart sick, whereas hope realised is like a tree of life.'

And I saw then that, despite all that counts against it, we must keep faith, trusting in the future – not just of our world but of ourselves, what life holds in store for *us*. For without hope there is no meaning, no life, no anything. Though dreams are dashed and confidence shattered, we must still believe that life can change; that next time will be different. For as daffodils bloom afresh in the springtime and swallows return once more, so will hope rise again, refusing to be denied. And as the nightingale sings even in the darkness, so shall our soul sing even through the deepest night.

I saw also that a person without hope is like a flame starved of oxygen, that a people without hope is like a field starved of water, that a world without hope is like a life starved of breath.

And I understood that hope alone makes fulfilment possible, holding out the prospect of change and the inspiration to keep on striving. Not vainly clutching at straws but rather daring to believe: a faith that in all the brokenness of humanity, all the aching heartbreak of this world, there is yet something precious, of infinite potential, that will somehow win through.

So then, however much you have been hurt, however often betrayed, however often disillusioned, nurture the seed of hope within you – the faith that good can come out of evil and joy out of sorrow – for only thus can we heal our broken world, turning its ugliness into a thing of beauty, its wilderness into a burgeoning of new life.

Humility

I saw a man full of his own importance, preening himself arrogantly, broadcasting his opinions for all to hear, sure of his own rightness.

I saw another, shy and retiring, cowed in a corner – awkward and embarrassed, studiously avoiding the eyes of all.

And my thoughts turned to humility: of how some need more of it and others need less.

So I said to the Teacher, 'What does it mean to be humble? Is it a weakness or a strength?'

And the Teacher answered, 'A proud heart leads to destruction, but humility earns true respect. When pride rears its head, embarrassment follows soon afterwards; those who are unassuming show true insight.'

Then I understood that humility is not just the absence of pride but the presence of something more: a balanced understanding of our strengths and weaknesses, a proper sense of who and what we are. For we all have both our good side and our bad, our fortes and our flaws, our beauty and our beast. Each has something to give to others and something to receive, something to teach and something to learn.

And I saw that humility means taking ourselves seriously yet being able to laugh at our foibles, standing by our convictions yet being open to those of others, exploring our potential yet recognising our limitations.

So I said to the Teacher, 'Instruct me further on this.'

And the Teacher said, 'Just as silver is refined in a crucible and gold in a furnace, so people are tested through being praised. If you have been so foolish as to exalt yourself, cover your mouth for shame.'

I understood then that there is no merit in thinking too much of ourselves . . . or too little; in puffing ourselves up or putting ourselves down; for neither false modesty nor vain posturing will make us any more or any less than we are.

I saw rather that humility means to hold our head up high, yet not to look down on others; to recognise our gifts yet never to trumpet them; to appreciate our worth but to appreciate that of others equally.

So then, my conclusion is this: whoever you are, *you* matter, but so do all who cross your path. Respect yourself as much as them, and them as much as yourself, and you will have got the balance right.

Integrity

I grinned self-consciously, swaggered, cowered, spoke out, kept quiet – each depending on who I was with, my persona changing according to the company I kept.

And I asked myself, confused, 'Which of these is me?' For I saw how swiftly I sway with the breeze, drifting now this way, now that, according to which way the wind is blowing.

Then I said to the Teacher, 'Speak to me about integrity. About truly being myself.'

And the Teacher answered, 'Those who preserve their integrity will protect their soul; those who surrender it consign themselves to a bottomless pit from which there is no escaping. Better not to have much and be true to yourself than to have all the riches in the world at the cost of your own integrity.'

Then I understood that to live fully we must first be able to live with *ourselves*, true to what lies within us. For though, like a reed, we must be willing to bend, flexible in our opinions and ready, where necessary, to change, yet we can never be all things to all people, for then we will be nothing to anyone. Better to be rejected for who we are than accepted for who we are not.

I recognised, likewise, the importance of living by our principles, ensuring that our words and deeds are consistent. For whoever says one thing and does another is like an unfaithful lover – not to be trusted and sure to be spurned – whereas those who practise what they preach, their answers honest and motives transparent, are like a harbour in a storm and an anchor in a tempest: a constant in a sea of change.

And I saw further that though we all wear many faces, depending on who we're with and where we find ourselves – and that each of these is part of who and what we are, a facet of the whole – we should never be *two-faced*, knowingly duplicitous, adopting one or the other guise for gain or comfort. For truly to be ourselves with another is the greatest compliment we can pay them, the deepest expression of trust and the surest key to friendship. And when we fail to be ourselves we sell not just them short but *us* as well.

So then, my counsel is this: pretend to be who you are not and you may lose sight of who you are. Better a semi-precious stone than a counterfeit diamond. Better the mundane that is real than a mirage in the desert. Better a mind at peace with itself than a self at peace with nothing.

Justice

I saw the news report – scenes of unimaginable suffering: families huddled in shanty towns, emaciated children dying in their hundreds, workers slaving for a pittance, communities driven from their homes – and I wept with sorrow at a world where most have so little and a few have so much.

'How can this be?' I asked the Teacher. 'Why do we let it happen?'

The Teacher answered, 'The field of the poor delivers bountiful produce, but injustice causes it to be swept away.'

And I realised that when one person feasts while another starves, there is no true justice, and while one sleeps easy while another has nowhere to lay their head, there can be no real peace. When one claims their rights but others are denied them, where riches for some means poverty for many, a storm lies brewing . . . a storm that will surely break.

And I saw too that though the roots of injustice may lie beyond us, and though we may feel powerless to make a difference, yet we can never wash our hands of it, for we are all complicit, part of a system that robs the poor to feed the rich, ignores the sick to pamper the healthy, crushes the weak to build up the strong.

Then I said to the Teacher, 'What can I do? Can this wrong ever be changed?'

And the Teacher said, 'The one who exploits the needy offends his maker, but happy is the one who is kind to the poor. To oppress the poor is to insult the one who created all. To show kindness to them is, in itself, an act of worship.'

'But I am only one person,' I protested, 'and their needs are so great. Their cries overwhelm me until I must shut them out.'

And the Teacher replied, 'If you shut your ears to the cry of the needy, when you call out in turn no one will hear you. Speak out for those denied a voice of their own; proclaim the rights of the destitute. Speak up and deal fairly; defend the rights of the poor and needy. For I have seen the tears of the oppressed, and they have no one to bring them comfort – for power and influence is loaded on the side of the oppressors.'

And I realised that just as we are part of the malaise, so we must be part of the cure; that justice depends not only on others but also on us. As well as *calling* for change, we must be ready to change in turn; as well as expecting others to play *their* part, we equally must play *ours*.

Truly, it is not enough simply to hope or pray for a time when justice is done, poverty is ended and none is needy; we must do what we can to bring that day closer, each being willing – in a world where so many go hungry – to have a little less so that they may at least have a little.

But I continued to question, asking, 'Can anything really change? Is not injustice endemic to our world, part of its warp and weave, rooted in powers and interests far greater than my own?'

Then the Teacher said, 'Those who sow injustice will reap disaster. Exploiting the poor in order to make oneself rich and to curry favour with the wealthy is ultimately the road to ruin.'

And I understood that, for all its strength, injustice will never triumph fully, for the human spirit will rise against it. For good is greater than evil and right greater than wrong, and though selfishness is strong, love will prove itself stronger.

My conclusion, then, is this: don't just talk of justice; seek it. Don't just bemoan exploitation; confront it. We cannot change the world alone, but together we can make a difference. Better surely to do a little than do nothing. Better to try and fail than never to try at all.

Laughter

I heard the sound of laughter, but it was cruel, sarcastic, teasing, and my heart ached for the one they mocked.

I heard laughter again, but it was weary and resigned, betraying pain as much as pleasure, melancholy rather than mirth.

I heard laughter a third time – warm, enriching, happy, speaking of enjoyment shared and spirits uplifted – and I knew that it was good.

So I said to the Teacher, 'Speak to me of what I have seen and heard.'

And concerning the first, the Teacher answered, 'The laughter of fools is like the crackling of kindling beneath a cooking pot, and like the hot air that rises from it. It is thoughtless to mock others, even if they appear to deserve it. Those who know better maintain a discreet silence.'

And I realised that laughing *at* others wounds and destroys, whereas laughing *with* them makes whole; that laughter shared is a tonic, but laughter abused is a poison.

'What then,' I asked, 'of those whose laughter seems hollow, who weep even as they smile?'

And the Teacher replied, 'Even when we laugh the heart can be sad, and when joy is over, sorrow remains. There is a time to laugh and a time to mourn.'

And I saw that laughter and tears are not strangers but cousins, for what brings happiness can also cause heartache, and what brings pleasure can also cause pain. And I saw that though some things are no laughing matter, we need to smile at them nonetheless, for only thus can we draw their sting.

Then I said, 'What of laughter from the heart? Of fun that uplifts and humour that unites?'

And the Teacher answered, 'A merry heart makes for a cheerful countenance, but a morose disposition crushes the spirit. Life seems wretched to those who are miserable; those with a cheerful heart, on the other hand, feast continually.'

I saw then that true laughter lightens our heart and brightens our spirit, for as food is to the body so is laughter to the soul. For when we see the funny side of life we see also its brighter side – the best even in the worst. And I discerned that a world without laughter is like a diamond without sparkle, a meal without savour, sunshine without warmth.

I saw too that laughter can have mighty results, in a moment turning anger to amusement, despair to delight and foe to friend; that what an argument cannot resolve a joke can placate, and what threatens to explode, a chuckle can defuse.

And I saw that if we would truly laugh with others, we must learn first to laugh ourselves, for if we fail to see the humour there we will misconstrue it everywhere.

So then, whenever you can, greet life with a smile and a little laughter, for when you do that, life will smile back at you. And whatever you do, never be too serious, for if you make that mistake, something is seriously wrong.

Laziness

I woke up late and laid in bed, telling myself that the job I had planned could wait a bit . . . till the next day . . . or the next . . . or the next. And somehow it never got done, along with a host of others. Yet, far from feeling rested by my indolence, I felt burdened by tasks weighing upon me, heavy as lead, crushing the breath from my body and life from my spirit.

And the Teacher approached me, saying, 'Consider the ant, you lazy thing; reflect on its busy lifestyle, and be wise. How much longer are you going to lie there, you idler? Beware of loving sleep too much, for otherwise you will become poor; wake up, and you will have more than enough of all you need.'

And I said to the Teacher, 'Leave me to rest longer. A few minutes more cannot hurt.'

Then the Teacher told me a story – short and simple: 'I passed by the field of one who was lazy, by the vineyard of someone with no sense; and I saw that it was all overrun with thistles; the ground strewn with weeds, and its stone wall in ruins. I took careful note of what I saw; I looked and received instruction. A quick doze, a brief nap, a little folding of the hands to rest, and poverty will come upon you like a thief, and penury like a brigand.'

'Surely you exaggerate,' I protested. 'Can this really be so?'

And the Teacher continued, 'The idle fail to plough when they should do; then, when the time for harvesting arrives, there is nothing to reap. Sow your seed in the morning, and keep busy even into the evening, for you have no way of knowing which of your labours will prosper. Maybe one will, maybe another – even perhaps both.'

Then I realised that if we would fulfil our potential and achieve our goals, we must work for them first, for without effort there can be no gain, without labour no reward. And I saw that what we often blame on circumstance can be down in fact to laziness, what we *fail* to do down to what we *failed* to do.

I understood further that what we put off until tomorrow hangs over us today, the knowledge of tasks undone returning to haunt us. Better to be ahead in our work than behind, for then we can relax not just in body but also in *mind*.

I saw also that nothing is more wearying than doing nothing; that idleness numbs rather than refreshes us, undermining the flesh and sapping the spirit.

So then, my conclusion is this: what we put *in* is what we get *out*. What we put *off* is what gets *left* out. Work first then, rest later, and the results may surprise you.

Loneliness

It was only a passing visit, just a brief call to say hello and check that she was well, but it was the highlight of her week, for she was alone and housebound, rarely seeing anybody from one day to the next. And as she opened the door, her face lit up with joy, as though she were greeting royalty.

Then I said to the Teacher, 'Speak to me of loneliness, of the cross so many carry.'

And the Teacher answered, 'There was a man with no family, entirely alone. He worked tirelessly, yet his eyes took no pleasure in the riches he amassed as a result. "Who am I doing all this for?" he asked himself. "Why am I denying myself the good time I could be having instead?"'

And I glimpsed the sense of emptiness that loneliness can bring: the feeling of futility, of each day being the same; of having no one to work for, to please, to share with – to make it all worthwhile.

I felt the weight of isolation, the pain of having love to share and no one to share it with, of feeling that your welfare matters to no one.

And I said to the Teacher, 'Speak more of this burden.'

Then the Teacher answered, 'Two are better than one; their efforts will bear fruit, for should one start to flag the other can step in and help them. It's bad news, though, for those who are on their own;

should they fall, there will be no one to lift them up. Two people can keep warm if they lie together. How, though, can we keep warm by ourselves? A single person will easily be overpowered, whereas two will be able to defend themselves. And a cord composed of *three* strands will not be broken in a hurry.'

I understood then the importance of company and the difference it makes to one's life. I glimpsed how special it is to share a conversation as much as a home, a meal as much a bed, a blessing as much as a burden, and sensed how vulnerable it must feel to be truly alone.

And I understood also that some feel isolated even in a crowd, trapped within themselves even when with others – perhaps the greatest loneliness of all. Yet I saw too that there are none so lonely as live only for themselves, and that if we keep the world at bay, we will always feel on our own. But if we will only reach out to the faceless crowd, we will find there are more than we might imagine who are as lonely as we are, yearning to find a friend.

And I saw that the surest cure for loneliness is not to *pine* for others, but to *think* of them, for no one is lonely when they offer solace. And to let someone who is on their own know that we care is like opening the door to their cage and helping them to fly.

So then, if you know someone who is lonely, reach out and let them know they matter, for by giving but a moment you can transform a whole day. And should you be the one alone, reach out likewise, and you may find a hand reaching out to you in turn.

Love

I saw a couple embracing, a mother hugging her child, a family sharing a meal, a friend reaching out to another, and love shone from them, a bond stronger than all others.

Yet I saw also the divorce papers, the abused child, the family feuds, the estranged friends, and I mourned that even love has its limits, feelings that had seemed so permanent falling like autumn leaves from the trees.

And I said to the Teacher, 'How can this be?'

And the Teacher replied, 'Hatred stirs up strife, but love covers over all offences. A simple meal seasoned with love is far better than the finest steak where there is also hatred. Never let go of love and faithfulness; wrap them around your neck and inscribe them deeply upon your heart.'

And I realised that true love does not bloom for a moment only to wilt and fade, but endures for ever, able to face the fiercest of storms, the bleakest of droughts, and still flourish. For it is able to see the worst yet look for the best; to meet with rejection yet keep on reaching out; to meet with change yet remain constant; to ask for nothing yet give all.

And I saw that though we may possess riches or status, without love we have nothing; and though we have insight and wisdom, without love we see nothing; and though we seek truth or virtue, without love we gain nothing; and though we may seem to have all, without love we *are* nothing. For while much may bring pleasure for a moment, love brings joy for a lifetime, and though other treasures may feed the mind and body, love nurtures the soul.

I saw that compared to love, all else is but an empty husk beside a priceless kernel, a shadow of the one thing needful. Yet I saw also how easily we replace this gift with pale substitutes – a moment's lust, a brief infatuation, a fleeting desire, a passing relationship – and I realised that though these may bring their own delight, love alone is the alchemy able to turn base metal into gold.

It gives, and goes on giving; cares, and goes on caring; believes, and goes on believing; seeking not its own welfare but the good of the one who's loved: no sacrifice too great, no expression of affection too small.

So then, my conclusion is this: seek love above all else, for it alone can truly satisfy, and if you would be loved, if you would foster love, if you would share love, then love first – wholly, deeply, truly – and all else will follow.

Patience

I saw an angler sprawled on a riverbank: no rush or bustle – just occasionally stirring to reel in his line and bait his hook afresh. And I was struck by the contrast with how so many of us live life, rushing from one thing to the next, always in a hurry, striving to cram that little bit extra into the unforgiving minute.

Then I said to the Teacher, 'Speak to me of patience and why it matters.'

And the Teacher answered, 'It is better to be patient in spirit than proud in spirit. Better to be patient than powerful. A task looks better on its conclusion than at its start.'

Then I saw the importance of waiting rather than expecting instant results – of saving before we spend, laying foundations before we build, tilling the ground before we sow – for when we act in haste, truly we will repent at leisure.

I saw further how the best results do not come in a moment: how mastering a craft takes years of practice, how learning involves hours of study, how a fine wine needs decades to mature, how an athlete spends months in training – patient preparation not being some optional extra but essential, integral to success. What takes longer to accomplish may be all the more satisfying to achieve; what we wait for is all the more special when it arrives.

Better to take things more gently, then, instead of dashing from one thing to the next, for a rushed job will likely be a poor job. Better to make haste slowly than hurry into a new venture and regret it afterwards, for the one who sets off too quickly rarely wins the race.

I saw likewise that those who seek short-term results may miss long-term blessings; that a bud picked early may never come to bloom, and fruit picked before it has ripened will invariably disappoint. For who would harvest a field when the crop has barely sprouted? And why cut down as a sapling what could later be felled as a tree? Is not the sowing as rewarding as the reaping? Is not scaling the mountain as fulfilling as attaining the summit? Truly, life is not just a destination but a journey, and the road we travel is as special as the place we strive to reach.

I saw also the importance of showing patience towards others: of giving them time to respond, to learn, to grow, if they are to attain their full potential. And I realised that when we lose our patience we lose also our friends, for why should they wait for us to find it again; why tarry for us if we will not tarry for them?

So then, however busy you may be, be patient, for there are few things that really can't wait. Make time to pause, to plan, to ponder, and you may find you have more time than you think. Better a job well done than a task half finished. Better a sip of wine tomorrow than a flagon of vinegar today.

Peace

I saw a world at war with itself, nation rising against nation, people against people, creed against creed and culture against culture, and I could see no end to it. For just as it is now, so it has been always – bloodshed and discord a recurring blot across the pages of history.

And I said to the Teacher, 'Show us a different way; a better path.'

And the Teacher answered, 'Whoever overlooks wrongdoing, dismissing it with a knowing wink, paves the way for trouble; whoever makes a principled stand against it ultimately paves the way for peace.'

Then I saw that to proclaim peace where there is no peace is simply to stoke the fires of conflict, and to paper over the cracks of division is merely to allow them to grow wider until they cannot be ignored.

For when nation oppresses nation there can be no resolution of discord; where people are exploited and injustice goes unchecked, no prospect of harmony; where poverty remains, and hunger, disease and squalor endure, no hope of concord; where country wages war against country or the aggrieved resort to bullet and bomb, no end to conflict.

And I saw that though one wrong does not make up for another, such a cycle of conflict and retribution is inevitable until the causes of division are addressed. For when a blind eye is turned to evil, it only grows stronger. And when injustice is ignored, its anger is multiplied.

I realised further that the causes of discord lie within us all – in our greed, ignorance, prejudice and fear – but so too do the seeds of its healing – in dialogue and openness, and standing up for right. For each is part of this world's brokenness, and each has a responsibility to work for its healing.

I saw, then, that we cannot leave to others what we must also do ourselves; that real change involves *us* changing too; and that to call for peace but fail to work for it is to whistle in the wind. For when we close our mind to injustice we close our heart to others. When we shrug our shoulders at wrong we collude in the crime. When we wink at the way of the world we condemn ourselves to walk it. When we fail to challenge evil we effectively condone it.

My conclusion, therefore, is this: do not just long for peace – think it, breathe it, live it. Where differences divide, challenge them; where waters are troubled, calm them; where chasms divide, bridge them; where wounds bleed, tend them. Let peace reign among us, and let it begin with you.

Prejudice

I saw a man mocked for his sexuality, children victimised for the colour of their skin, a community persecuted for its faith, a woman passed over on account of her gender, and I knew that thousands endure such prejudice each day, their lives blighted by bigotry and intolerance.

So I said to the Teacher, 'Speak to me of prejudice.'

And the Teacher answered, 'As a saying of the wise has it: a prejudiced judgement is never good.'

Then I understood that prejudice should have no place among us, for it is a canker that denigrates and divides, reducing people to objects, categories, labels, no longer deserving of respect or dignity but to be dismissed, derided, even destroyed.

And I saw how prejudice stems from ignorance – not just a failure to understand but a refusal even to try; a hiding behind walls of dogma to avoid engaging with possibilities we'd rather not face. For what is prejudice but a closing of the mind and shuttering of the spirit; a rejection of the need to justify a position or argue a point – association alone being enough to condemn without a hearing, case closed before any evidence is even considered.

Yet I understood that this says more about the one prejudiced than the one discriminated against; more about the insecurity, fear and hatred that drives bigotry than the recipients of its poison. For none can be judged by colour or creed, class or culture. All are unique and precious, just as all are flawed and foolish.

Then I said to the Teacher, 'What feeds our prejudice, and why does it continue?'

And the Teacher answered, 'It is wrong to be prejudiced towards some or biased against others, but people will stoop to both for a mere crust of bread.'

And I recognised that we use prejudice to further our own ends: to reinforce our status and identity at the cost of others; to put ourselves among the in-crowd, the 'normal', and to push others outside; to label as right or wrong, good or bad, with no doubt left as to which side we are on.

And none is immune, for prejudice lurks in us all: in our easy assumptions, our lazy jumping to conclusions, our all-too-ready passing of judgement; in our perceiving differences as a threat rather than invitation to dialogue, and our closing our ears to whatever questions our preconceptions. Afraid or unwilling to risk genuine encounter, we pigeonhole those who challenge or unsettle us, determined to keep our distance.

My conclusion, then, is this: look not at the labels we place upon others, but at the person beneath, recognising that prejudice runs deeper than we may think, even within our very soul. Approach others as you would have them approach you, respect if you would be respected, and look not for the worst in all, but the best.

Pride

I looked a fool, and I felt like one, for I'd rashly boasted of my abilities and been found wanting. 'Leave it with me,' I'd said. 'It's easy when you know how.' But it wasn't easy, for I didn't know how at all, my confidence swiftly being exposed as empty conceit.

Then I said to the Teacher, 'Instruct me concerning the perils of pride.'

And the Teacher answered, 'Someone who promises much but delivers nothing is like a cloud rolling in that fails to produce rain. Pride goes before our undoing, and an arrogant spirit before a fall. An individual's pride will lead to them falling flat on their face, but whoever is humble in spirit will receive respect.'

Then I understood that the more inflated our opinion is of ourselves, the more likely it is to burst. And I saw that setting ourselves up on a pedestal only increases the likelihood of falling, and the greater the claims we make, the greater will be our humiliation should we fail to live up to them. Better to be brought down a peg or two today than to crash down to earth tomorrow.

Then I said to the Teacher, 'Is there no place, then, for pride?'

And the Teacher answered, 'A supercilious attitude and a proud heart – trademarks of evildoers – are equally wrong. It is better humbly to take a seat among the poor than to divide the spoil with the proud.'

Then I saw that though there is a place for pride in our achievements, there is never one for vanity, for empty claims are worthless, diminishing those who make them.

And I saw that though all should value themselves, none should value themselves too highly. And though all should hold their head up high, none should lift theirs higher than others, looking down on those around them. For we are all children of creation, each having a right to be here.

I saw too that arrogance makes many boasts, but few friends, and that to think ourselves better than others is to make ourselves worse.

'Show me, then, how to avoid pride,' I urged the Teacher, 'how to keep a balanced perspective of who and what I am.'

And the Teacher answered, 'Let someone else flatter you, not your own mouth – someone you don't know rather than your own lips.'

And I realised that if we blow our own trumpet, it will always be out of tune, sounding a discordant note that shatters harmony and sets the teeth on edge; that it is better to make music together than perform a solo no one wants to hear.

I saw too that though we may not like how others perceive us, the picture they have of us is probably more accurate than that which we have of ourselves. For while we may be fooled by what our ego is telling us, they will be less easily taken in.

And I saw that arrogance serves only to feed our misplaced yearning for approbation; that true friends love us not for what we claim to be but for what we are.

So then, my conclusion is this: do not think too little of yourself, but neither too much. Better to be raised up than put down, to stand in another's shoes and see ourselves from their point of view than to get too big for our boots. For pride leads not only to a fall, but to a *fool*.

Quarrelling

I watched the quarrel unfold, and it was all so unnecessary, so foolish, for it was just a disagreement to begin with, nothing more – a mere difference of opinion – and that should have been an end to it, each putting the incident behind them and moving on. But both, feeling piqued, were determined to prove a point, so they dug their heels in and refused to give ground, until that little dispute became a raging argument – dividing, undermining, estranging.

Then I said to the Teacher, 'Instruct me concerning quarrels and how to avoid them.'

And the Teacher answered, 'Starting a quarrel is like springing a leak. Stop, then, before a dispute turns nasty. Avoid arguing with someone unless you have very good reason, and especially if no harm has been done to you.'

And I saw that though a quarrel may be justified it is rarely helpful, and even where it is helpful it is rarely worth prolonging, for instead of bringing together it drives people apart, instead of fostering agreement it engenders discord, instead of encouraging debate it stifles discussion, each protagonist ending up saying things they didn't mean in a way they never meant to say them.

Then I asked the Teacher, 'Why do quarrels so quickly get out of hand?'

And the Teacher replied, 'Fools are invariably swift to quarrel; by far the more honourable course is to avoid discord. A fire short of wood soon dies. Likewise a quarrel swiftly ends where there is no one to stoke it up. In much the same way as smouldering embers respond to charcoal and fire to wood, so is an argumentative person in terms of kindling strife.'

And I saw that the fiercer the argument, the more the cause of it is forgotten, most quarrels becoming about standing one's ground, saving face and proving oneself to be the stronger, never mind the rights or wrongs.

I saw also that though it may take two to start an argument, it needs only one to keep it going. And though some points are sufficiently important to defend, they are fewer than we might think, not many being worth quarrelling about, still less falling out over.

The lesson I have learnt is this: better to be thought wrong than to insist on your rightness. Better to douse a quarrel than to fan the flames. Better, above all, to lose a quarrel than lose a friend.

Relationships

I stood and watched the crowds go by, a nameless sea of faces, and I realised how much we need relationships – family, friends, colleagues – to give us a sense of identity and belonging – a sense of place in this world.

Then I said to the Teacher, 'Speak more to me concerning relationships, of how they shape our lives.'

And the Teacher answered, 'Iron can be used to sharpen iron; likewise one person helps to hone the character of another.'

I saw then that just as pebbles on the beach are made smooth through grinding together in the waves, so rubbing shoulders with others helps to knock off our rough edges, rounding us as individuals.

And I understood our need to mix with people of different convictions, backgrounds and temperaments in order to challenge our preconceptions and broaden our horizons – those able to offer new ways of looking at life and thus of understanding ourselves. For when we gravitate only to those of a like mind, we stop our world from expanding and ourselves from maturing, seeing only what we want to see and hearing only what we want to hear.

And I saw that when we fail to look outwards we turn inwards, ever more entrenched in our opinions and fixed in our ways.

I saw further how our relationships help to shape the people we are – how those whom we like prove to be those we *become* like, *their* ways turning into *our* ways and their views into our views. Watch, then, the company you keep if you would continue to be happy with your own company, for those you mix with will change you more than you might imagine – for good or for ill.

I realised also that just as we need others, they need us; that as they shape our lives, so we shape theirs. And my head reeled at the privilege yet responsibility this brings: our potential to influence a life for better or worse – to impoverish or enrich, bless or blight, help or harm.

I saw above all the importance in any relationship of being true both to ourselves and to the other, for without mutual respect there is no real coming together, no meaningful connection or lasting bond. Truly, though partners in any relationship may change, if we make such change a condition of its success then already it is doomed to failure, for if we cannot love someone for who they are we will never love them at all.

Make time, then, for others – not just those you find it easy to get along with but also those you find it hard, not just those you agree with but equally those you don't. Work at your relationships and, above all, celebrate them, for just as a problem shared is a problem halved and a joy shared is a joy doubled, so a life touched by another is a life deepened, enriched beyond measure.

Religion

I saw theologians debating, clerics arguing, schisms separating, zealots persecuting – and I grieved at such a denial of what was supposedly held dear. Yet I saw also believers campaigning for justice, serving their community, working together to restore and reconcile – and for a moment faith was restored.

'What, then, of religion?' I asked. 'How has it brought such joy, yet such sorrow; such insight, yet such bigotry; such good, yet such evil; such blessing, yet such a curse?'

And the Teacher reminded me that the divine is beyond words, greater than we can ever comprehend, let alone confine to creed or dogma: 'God is greater than any human being, towering above us in majesty; who can begin to be anything like such a tutor? Who has decreed the way God should take, or who can say, "You have done wrong"? Surely the divine is so awesome that we can never know it fully; the number of its years is beyond our reckoning.'

'So can we not know God?' I asked. 'Is religion a folly, a deceit, an illusion?'

'God has made everything beautiful in its time,' answered the Teacher with a shake of the head, 'and has put a glimpse of eternity in the human heart.

Yet no one is able fully to fathom everything that God has done.'

'What, then, can we say of God?' I asked. 'For much has been written, and many claim that theirs and theirs alone is the way to truth. And of doctrine and teaching there seems to be no end.'

Then the Teacher answered me, 'When in the presence of the divine, avoid being over-hasty to speak, in a hurry to blurt out whatever comes into your mind. Given that God is in heaven and you are on earth, let your words be few. Much dreaming and many words are empty. Therefore, stand in awe before God.'

And I understood then that religion has a place, but that it must know its place too; that it is a searching after truth, never a quest that is finished. And I realised that whenever religion claims to be wholly right, it is deeply wrong; that it is better to have no religion than to believe ours is the only one worth having; and that in striving to protect truth, religion often destroys it, as much obscuring as revealing the face of God.

And what is the face of God but the face of love? Without love, religion is nothing: like night without day – a tyrant that brings death in the name of the giver of life. And those who condemn in the name of faith, who persecute and destroy, demean not just themselves but also the God they claim to worship.

Truly, there is nothing worth killing for, least of all religion, and though some things are worth dying for, religion is not among them.

So then, hold fast to God, but hang loose to religion, and never confuse the two.

Remorse

I saw a workman struggling with his load, veins knotted on his brow and sweat dripping down his cheeks, until finally he could carry it no longer and he laid it down, glad of a moment's rest.

And I was reminded of how we can carry baggage of a different sort through life: staggering under a burden of guilt, a weight of remorse – our faults and mistakes ever before us, denying us peace.

Then I said to the Teacher, 'Speak to me of error, of how to live with wrongdoing.'

And the Teacher answered, 'Those who do wrong are haunted by guilt, always on the brink of taking flight, even though no one is pursuing them.'

Then I understood how our mistakes bring their own punishment, how guilt stalks us in the darkness, whispering its forbidden secrets, confronting us with the spectre of our true self laid bare.

And I saw how, if not addressed, such remorse hangs over us, condemning us to walk in shadow while others savour the sun.

Then I said to the Teacher, 'How should we deal with guilt? Can we ever escape it?'

And the Teacher answered, 'Not a single person on earth is perfect, nor is there anyone who invariably does what is good and never makes a mistake. Who can claim, "I have cleansed my heart from evil; I have purified myself from wrongdoing"? No one who conceals mistakes will prosper, but whoever confesses and turns from them will obtain mercy.'

Then I realised that no one is without blemish; that all fall short. And I realised also that if we would be free from guilt we must be truly penitent, not just *feeling* sorry but *saying* so, and not just *saying* sorry but *being* so. For though 'sorry' is truly hard to say, it is but a word, and words cost little whereas actions cost much.

I saw too that remorse is worth nothing unless it is matched by a desire to make amends. For though we cannot make up for every wrong or undo the consequences of our actions, the extent to which we try demonstrates the sincerity of our contrition. And though recognising our mistakes is a start, it is turning from them that makes a difference, both to us and to those we've wronged.

I saw also that remorse that wallows in self-pity is not remorse at all; that seeking solely to assuage our guilt merely compounds a wrong rather than puts it right. For though *we* may need healing of our guilt, others need healing of a greater hurt, and our duty is first to them and only second to ourselves.

My conclusion, then, is this: better to face up to our mistakes than wait for them to catch up with us. Better to say sorry now than be sorrier later. Better to seek forgiveness and have it denied than never to seek it at all.

Rest

I saw a man working all hours of the day – slaving from dawn till dusk – intent on achieving success and indulging himself in riches. But I couldn't help wondering whether he'd live to see them, or be able to relax enough to enjoy them if he did.

Then I said to the Teacher, 'Speak to me of work and rest, of getting the balance right.'

And the Teacher answered, 'Those who work their land will have sufficient for their daily needs; those who fritter away their time are foolish. Hard work brings its own reward.'

I understood, then, that work is not just a necessity but a privilege, for through labour, whatever it may be, we gain dignity, each contributing a thread to the rich tapestry of life. And through our toil we secure not only our daily bread but also our identity, discovering more of who we are.

'What, then, of rest?' I asked. 'Which matters most?'

And the Teacher answered, 'Better to enjoy a handful with some well-earned rest than to win two handfuls through constant toil; that is ultimately a striving vainly after the wind.'

Then I realised that if work is sacred, so too is leisure, each being part of a life well lived; that there is more to life than the acquisition of possessions or pursuit of success, but more also than rest and relaxation, for just as work without leisure is meaningless toil, so leisure without work is empty indulgence.

And I understood that we must learn the difference between doing enough and doing too much, for if we fail to unwind we will end up no good for anything. Truly, there are times when, however weary we may be and however difficult we find it to continue, we must persevere with the task in hand, seeing it through to completion. But truly, likewise, there are times when, whatever we think needs doing and however vital it may seem, we must learn to let go, or all will pay the price.

Better to leave a job unfinished than be undone by it. Better to have a little in life than no time truly to live. Better to savour the breeze than chase after the wind.

What I conclude, therefore, is this: do what needs to be done, but recognise also what doesn't yet need doing. Make time for work but also for rest, for action but also for reflection, for others but also for yourself, and learn to keep each in its proper place.

Revenge

I saw the scenes at the football match: hooligans kicking, punching, wrestling, brawling – and when they were led away, the fight finally broken up, I saw hatred in their eyes, a determination to get even with their foe.

I saw the person slighted, belittled in front of their peers, and heard them mutter darkly of getting their own back, of being avenged.

Then I said to the Teacher, 'Speak to me of vengeance and to what it leads.'

And the Teacher answered, 'Never say, "I will do to others what they have done to me; I will get my own back and make them pay."'

And I was chastened, for I saw that the words applied to me as much as to anyone, that none of us is exempt. For though most refrain from violence, the thirst for revenge lurks deep within us all, and when we are wronged, aggrieved, disparaged, we want redress: an eye for an eye and a tooth for a tooth.

But I saw the folly of such a path: how revenge sets in motion a chain hard to break, demanding that we wound as we have been wounded, hurt as we have been hurt, punish as we have been punished – an endless cycle of tit for tat and blow for blow. I saw how vengeance leads to more vengeance and bitterness to more bitterness, swelling the tide of resentment and thirst for retribution. And I saw how a hunger for revenge destroys *us* as much as the one we seek to punish, gnawing like a moth at our very soul.

So I asked the Teacher, 'How can we stem these waters, prevent the trickle from becoming a flood?'

And the Teacher answered, 'If an enemy is hungry, offer them something to eat. If they are thirsty, give them a drink. For in doing so you will pile burning coals on their head.'

I understood then that if revenge reinforces hatred, a generous spirit questions it, and that when we return evil with good, an enemy can become a friend. For though vengeance may be justified and our thirst for it natural, forgiveness opens the way to new beginnings.

And I saw that if we would further peace rather than discord we must meet violence with nonviolence, hatred with love, cruelty with kindness, and anger with gentleness, for no fire burns when starved of fuel.

The lesson, surely, is this: love though you are not loved, forgive though you are not forgiven, care though you are not cared for, give though you do not receive. Act towards others not as they've acted towards you, but as you would have them do so, and perhaps they too will learn to do the same.

Sensitivity

I saw people offering counsel, well-meaning but misguided – telling the depressed to pull themselves together, the sick to have more faith, the bereaved to look on the bright side, the deprived to think themselves lucky. And I marvelled at such insensitivity, at how hard we find it to stand in another's shoes and glimpse something of their lot.

And I said to the Teacher, 'Speak to me of empathy, of why we find it so hard.'

And the Teacher answered, 'Each heart discerns its own bitterness, and nobody else can fully share its joy.'

And I realised how little we can understand of others, and how difficult it is to discern what they're going through. For their pain is not our pain, their sorrow not our sorrow, their testing not our testing, their life not our life. However much we understand of them, it will only be the tiniest fraction, a distorted reflection in a murky pool, and to assume more is foolish arrogance and a dangerous self-deception.

I realised also that though few of us would hurt someone intentionally, we *do* hurt them nonetheless, insensitive words or thoughtless deeds wounding the spirit if not the body, and causing untold harm.

So I said to the Teacher, 'How, then, can we avoid this? Teach me how to show compassion.'

And the Teacher answered, 'What someone means and desires in their heart is deep water indeed, but those with genuine insight will slowly draw it out. To offer good advice appropriate to the circumstances is like giving someone a silver basket full of golden apples. How special it is to offer a word in season – a joy to all concerned!'

And I realised that like balm on a wound, water on a fire, ice on a bruise, so is one who cares enough to draw close to us, to stand alongside and listen, offering not platitudes but words from the heart, not easy answers but genuine concern.

I saw also the importance of pausing before speaking, listening before answering, considering before pronouncing, assessing before advising. For what we think we know of someone and what we actually know are rarely the same, most of us jumping to conclusions on the flimsiest of evidence, our response saying more about us than the one we presume to help.

So then, my counsel is this: before you open your mouth, open your mind. Before you jump in, consider to whom you are speaking. And in all you say or do, think of them first, yourself second.

Sorrow

They stood by the graveside weeping, and they were overwhelmed, broken, for their loved one had been taken from them, their joy sealed in a coffin.

And I knew that these were just some of a multitude who mourn and weep, walking in the shadow of loss, of hurt, of sorrow and suffering. And it seemed as though the world would drown in tears that none could wipe away.

Then I asked the Teacher, 'Talk to me concerning grief: of how to bear it.'

And the Teacher answered, 'Sorrow eats away at the human heart as surely as a moth gnaws at clothing or a worm nibbles wood.'

Then I understood that a broken heart is not easily mended, for each day brings memories that break it afresh. Though time may indeed heal many wounds, the ache of loss will always be there, for if joy warms like a blanket, sorrow hangs chill as a shroud, bereft of life, devoid of hope.

And I saw that though accepting the reality of loss is painful, denying it will hurt us more, since it is only through confronting the awfulness of heartbreak that we can draw its sting and blunt its claws. For what we run from will patiently stalk us, and what we hide from will forever seek us out.

Then I said to the Teacher, 'Is there no way to reduce sadness, no lesson you can give?'

And the Teacher answered, 'The more we learn the more we have cause to grieve, for with much wisdom and knowledge also comes much sorrow.'

And I realised that the more we understand, the more we weep, for we discern the tragedy within the beauty of life: the thorns that belie the rosebuds, that flaw that mars the diamond.

I saw also that without sorrow there can be no joy, without tears no laughter, without pain no pleasure. For what is plenty but the absence of shortfall? And what is darkness but a lack of light? Where joy has not been tasted it can never be missed, and where the sun does not shine there can be no shadow. Better to know grief alongside rejoicing than never to have rejoiced at all.

So then, if you would avoid tasting sorrow do not expect joy, for the two are twins, conceived in the same womb – and to shut out one is to exclude the other. If you would laugh, learn also to weep; if you would rejoice, learn also to mourn; for they are two sides of the one coin, fashioned from the same metal, stamped in the same press. The chalice of grief cannot be sweetened, but from the same cup comes the wine of joyfulness, life's draughts of delight, and if you would live fully you must drink deeply of both.

Time

I heard the sound of the alarm clock, shrill and strident; of my watch ticking quietly on my wrist; of church bells chiming, announcing the passing of another hour. And my thoughts turned to the mystery of time: how when life is good, we want it to stand still; when life is busy, we want more of it; when life is dull, we don't know what to do with it; and when life is hard, it seems never to end.

So I said to the Teacher, 'Speak to me of how to use time wisely, how to understand it.'

And the Teacher answered, 'There is a season for everything, and a time for every activity under heaven: a time to be born and a time to die; a time to plant and a time to uproot; a time to kill and a time to heal; a time to pull down and a time to build up; a time to cry and a time to laugh; a time to grieve and a time to dance; a time to scatter stones and a time to gather them; a time to embrace and a time not to embrace; a time to seek and a time to lose; a time to keep and a time to throw away; a time to tear and a time to mend; a time for silence and a time for speech; a time to love and a time to hate; a time for war and a time for peace.'

Then I understood that there is indeed a time and place for everything in life, and that the secret is to grasp the moment, whatever it may be, and live it to the full, whether it brings joy or sorrow, pleasure or pain, fulfilment or disappointment. For truly not just *some* moments are precious, but *all* of them, if only we have eyes to see. Yet, while all has its place in due season, yesterday is yesterday and tomorrow is tomorrow, and neither must intrude on today.

But I saw equally how often we waste time or use it unwisely. How we *have* time but fail to recognise it. How we chase time, losing it in our haste to get things done. How we resist time, attempting to refute what can never be denied. How we squander time, forgetting in the humdrum business of life simply to live.

So I said to the Teacher, 'Where do we go wrong? Is there one lesson to learn above the rest?'

And the Teacher answered, 'Those who are in too much of a hurry miss the way.'

I saw then that so little of what we do is as pressing as we think, and that too easily – in the demands and responsibilities of another day – we lose touch with the simple but special things in life: those that really matter. For though there's a time for busyness, for doing instead of simply talking, there's a time also for being still and reflecting on what really counts. And though some things can't be put off until tomorrow, others don't need doing today, so learn to step back a little, and to think about what you're doing and why.

So, then, my conclusion is this: do not fritter your time away, for it is the most precious of gifts, and once gone you can never claw it back. Do not fear time, seeking to halt its progress, for that is to deny ourselves its joys as we run from its sorrows. Live each moment unto itself, and strive not to fill the unforgiving minute, for if we have no time to pause and ponder, to reflect and take stock, we have no time ultimately for anything.

Truth

I saw a preacher on a street corner, proclaiming 'the truth' to passers-by – and devil take those who disagreed. I saw the politician giving an interview, adamant that he spoke the truth yet proving economical with it at best. I saw churchgoers arguing with each other, each insisting theirs was the real truth and the other's a heresy. I saw pictures of the terrorist attack, justified supposedly in the name of truth.

And my soul recoiled in anger and despair, for each was genuine, and each was wrong.

Then I said to the Teacher, 'What is truth? So many claim it as theirs, but can we ever know it?'

And the Teacher answered, 'A falsehood has a fleeting life, whereas truth lives on for ever. Get hold of truth and never sell it. Do not lose your grip on truth or love: tie them around your neck and inscribe them upon the tablet of your heart.'

Then I understood that we must seek for truth as for treasure, for without it falsehood will go unchallenged. Yet I saw too that truth and love go hand in hand, each being part of the other, and that without love there is no truth, for if truth is the absence of error then falsehood is the absence of love. And I saw that without love we are nothing, without love there *is* nothing; that we are loved and made for love.

So then, to limit truth to doctrine or dogma is folly and arrogance, a setting ourselves up as God when we are all too human. Such is the path to perdition, the way of tyrants masked as saints.

For love is the one truth needful, and without it all else is flawed. What is true for me may be false for you, and what is right today may be wrong tomorrow. Where one sees good, another sees evil; where some glimpse light, others perceive darkness. None of us has the truth, the whole truth and nothing but the truth, and only the foolish presume otherwise.

Live faithfully, then, by what you believe, but do not insist upon your way. Stand up for your convictions but do not condemn those who may not share them. Seek insight and wisdom, but never assume your journey is complete, destination reached. Let love be your truth, your creed, your lodestone, and you will not go far wrong.

Wealth

I saw the queue for the lottery tickets, longer than I'd ever seen it before, for the jackpot was a record high, inspiring visions of unimaginable wealth, riches that would change life for ever. No more work, no more worries – the house and lifestyle of one's dreams.

And I understood the excitement, for although money doesn't necessarily buy happiness, it certainly contributes towards it, and when money is tight, happiness is frequently in equally short supply.

So I said to the Teacher, 'Speak to me of wealth, of the place it should have in our life.'

And the Teacher answered, 'Do not exhaust yourself in an effort to get rich; be sensible enough to avoid that trap, for though you see it one minute, it will disappear the next, suddenly taking wings to itself and flying off into the sky like an eagle. The miser rushes to get rich, apparently ignorant of the fact that loss is sure to come. The wealthy believe their riches to be like a fortified city; they picture their plenty as a mighty wall. But riches do not last for ever.'

And I was reminded that worldly wealth, like so much else, is transient, here today and gone tomorrow; that though affluence offers blessings few would decline, much of what it seems to bestow is illusory, unable really to satisfy, let alone meet our deepest needs. For though we are materially rich we may be spiritually poor, seeming to have everything yet in fact having nothing.

But I knew that the same is true of much else this life has to offer, so I pressed the Teacher further. 'Surely,' I urged, 'riches add to happiness. No one could argue with that.'

Then the Teacher answered, 'Those who love money will never be satisfied by money alone, neither will those who love wealth be content with whatever they acquire.'

I saw then that the more we have the more we seem to want, yet the less we seem to appreciate it; that riches do not always correspond with richness, nor a full wallet with a full life. And I saw too that there are some things we cannot buy – that, truly, the best things in life are free: the embrace of love, a heart at peace, a healthful body, a happy home – gifts beyond purchase, beyond price.

So I said to the Teacher, 'How, then, should wealth be handled?'

And the Teacher answered, 'Those who give to the poor will find their own needs provided in turn, but curses on those who ignore them.'

I saw then that wealth brings responsibility as well as luxury: to ease the plight of the needy, to respond to those less fortunate, to make a difference for good. And I saw too that riches come not just from the sweat of a single brow, but equally from the labour of others, the toil, vision and effort of the many who make it possible. What these have put in, so they should take out; to each their due reward.

And I saw that compared to many, most of us have enough and more than enough, and that when we learn to give generously from our plenty we will discover what enrichment really means.

But wealth that is hoarded away, jealously guarded by hook or by crook, is not wealth at all but a poverty of mind and spirit, a manacle on the soul. Better for our purse to be empty than our heart. Better to be content with little than ceaselessly to strive after more. Better to make money our servant than to be its slave.

What I have learned, then, is this: do not despise wealth nor resent it, but do not worship it either, for though it can feed the body it cannot nourish the soul. Pursue money by all means, but not at the cost of all else, or what you seek to consume will consume you instead. And whatever riches you have, use them wisely, not just for your own benefit but for that of others too. For when we can give as we have received, deny ourselves to bless another, then we are truly wealthy.

Wisdom

I looked at the world around me and saw what seemed to be madness, for there was war and hatred, poverty and hardship, evil and exploitation, sorrow and suffering, and for all our resources and progress, none could agree on how to solve them.

I saw also peace and prosperity, plenitude and privilege, yet even with all this, people seemed lost, searching for answers and yearning for meaning.

And I said to the Teacher, 'How is it that we seek yet do not find? Where should we look for understanding – for an insightful and discerning spirit?'

Then the Teacher said to me, 'Obtain wisdom; cultivate insight. Though you forget everything else I tell you, do not forget this. Fools clothe themselves with folly, but the wise are crowned with discernment.'

So I asked, 'Where should we seek this wisdom? Of what does it consist?'

And the Teacher replied, 'The secret of becoming wise can be summed up thus: acquire wisdom! Above all else, seek insight. Value her highly, and she will lift you up; hold tight to her and she will exalt you, placing a beautiful garland upon your head; a glorious crown.'

'But many seek wisdom,' I answered, 'yet not all find it. Explain this to me.'

'Sensible people gain knowledge,' responded the Teacher; 'wise ears search for understanding. It is stupid and reprehensible to have an answer ready for someone before you've even listened to what they've got to say. Whoever first puts forward a case appears to be right, until someone else comes along and cross-examines them.'

'Tell me more,' I urged. 'Teach me further about such wisdom.'

And the Teacher said, 'Unless they are guided wisely, people lose their way; the more shrewd counsel they listen to, the better will be their chances. Only a fool believes they are always right; the wise value advice. If you are prepared to take advice and learn from it, then, in time, you will grow wise.'

'Speak, and help me to listen,' I said. 'Share with me what you have learnt.'

And the Teacher smiled, and answered, 'When I applied myself to acquiring wisdom, and to understanding the workings of this world of ours, I glimpsed the hand of God, and realised that no one can fully fathom what is taking place beneath the sun. However much effort anyone may put into their search, they cannot unravel the mystery of life; despite the claims of those who profess wisdom, no one can discover it. What I have concluded is this: though I say to myself, "I will become wise," wisdom continues to escape me. That which is truly real is distant, profound and unfathomable; can anyone ever fully discover it?'

I pondered these words, and realised that the genuinely wise are those who recognise how little they have understood; that the more we discover, the more there is yet to be explored; the more we grasp, the more still eludes us.

And I realised that wisdom lies not in being certain, but in being open; not in having all the answers but in having many questions; not in believing we are right but in accepting we may be wrong. For wise are those who see their own ignorance, and shallow are those who think themselves deep.

I saw too that the path to wisdom lies not in the accumulation of many facts but in the gathering of much experience; not just in learning from books but in learning from others; not only in opening the mind but also in opening the heart – in contemplating the mysteries of life, the awesomeness of the universe and the wonder of the divine with eyes that see and ears that hear.

So, then, my counsel is this: seek wisdom, but never conclude you have found it, for assuredly then you have not. Seek insight, but never think it complete, for unquestionably then it isn't. Better to think you know less than you do than to assume you know more; to understand only a little than to misunderstand much.

Words

I looked at the page and saw words: special and deep – designed to bless, heal, encourage and nurture.

I looked again and saw more words: mean and spiteful – aimed to wound, belittle, degrade and destroy.

And I marvelled at how what seem so innocent can bring so much good yet so much evil – how words can delight or dismay, enrich or enrage, enlighten or obscure, affirm or deny.

Then I said to the Teacher, 'Help me to understand words better and to use them more wisely. Show me their good and their bad, their potential yet pitfalls.'

And the Teacher answered, 'Words both kill and give life; we reap the consequences of what we say. Pleasing words are like honey, bringing health to the body and sweetness to the soul. Reckless words are like sword thrusts, but a wise tongue brings healing. Those who are prudent watch their tongues; those who speak without thinking come to ruin.'

And I understood the awesomeness yet awfulness of words: their power to foster love and life yet to be wielded as weapons of war; their capacity to let us play angel or demon, friend or foe.

I saw the beauty of words: how they can enchant and amaze, excite and enthral, articulating the deepest of emotions and profoundest of thoughts. But I saw also their ugliness: the ways in which we lash out through them, intent on wounding, deliberately cruel – how we use them to hurt, deceive, ridicule or revile; to incite hatred and intolerance, violence and war. And I realised that words must be handled with care, for once uttered they cannot be taken back.

I saw also that from the same mouth proceeds both blessing and curse, wisdom and folly, for few can master the tongue and few are not its slaves.

So I said to the Teacher, 'How, then, should we speak?'

And the Teacher answered, 'The more you have to say, the more likely you are to cause harm by saying the wrong thing; the sensible course is to speak less and think more. Whoever uses words sparingly is wise; the discerning remain measured in what they say. Even the most stupid person who keeps their own counsel is considered astute; so long as their lips stay firmly sealed, they are reckoned shrewd. But there is more hope for a fool than for someone who blurts out words without thinking.'

Then I saw that it is better to keep silent than to open one's mouth without thinking, for what we say in haste we will repent of at leisure, and what we think will not hurt can cut deepest of all. And I saw that it is wiser likewise to say nothing than to knowingly cause harm.

Better, though, to use our tongue wisely than hold it altogether; to put to good what others put to evil, and to employ to heal what others employ to harm. For to speak kindly and with love is to plant flowers among thistles, and to bring forth fruit from among thorns.

My conclusion, then, is this: consider carefully how you use your tongue, for small as it is, its power is great, for good or for ill. Harness your tongue, but do not bridle it completely. Consider your words, but do not withhold them all. Guard your lips, but do not seal your mouth. Let your speech be pure as the morning dew, refreshing as a summer's shower, warm as the midday sun, bringing health and wholeness to all.

Epilogue

I have pondered long and hard on the mysteries of life, but am I nearer to answers than when I first began? I have looked for wisdom, searched for understanding, but am I closer to finding it? For all my musings, any insights I may have gained seem as fleeting as the breeze, ephemeral as the morning mist.

For every argument there is a refutation. For every plus, a minus. Always there is more to puzzle over, more to ask. What I have debated, others have considered before me. What I have concluded, others will question. No answer is complete, no judgement accepted as final.

So I said to the Teacher, 'Has my search been in vain? You have taught me much yet I fathom so little. You have spoken of understanding yet still I am mystified.'

The Teacher nodded knowingly at this, then answered with a smile, 'Who among us is truly wise? Who knows the explanation of things?'

And I realised that it is not those who think they have all the answers who are wise, but those who dare to ask questions, and that it is not doubt we need to fear but certainty: the bigot who will not listen and the zealot who refuses to think. Truly, a little knowledge is a dangerous thing, yet which of us has more?

So then, seek wisdom, though you will always fall short; search for insight, though it will constantly run ahead of you. For if we never seek we will never find; if we never find we will never learn; if we never learn we will never grow; and if we never grow we will never fully live.

References

Anxiety

'How special is the light of each
   new day . . .'   Ecclesiastes 11:7

'A wise person always keeps an eye
   open for possible problems . . .'   Proverbs 27:12, 1

'A word of encouragement helps
   to cheer people up . . .'   Proverbs 12:25

Contentment

'How happy are those with
   discernment . . .'   Proverbs 3:13-15

'It is better to honour God . . .'   Proverbs 15:16

'Better to be poor and upright . . .'   Proverbs 16:8

'And better to feed peaceably . . .'   Proverbs 17:1

'I ask for two things only before
   I die . . .'   Proverbs 30:7, 8

Criticism

'A wise criticism is like a
   gold ring . . .'   Proverbs 25:12

'Whoever takes note of good
   advice . . .'   Proverbs 10:17

'Anyone who ignores wise counsel
   despises themselves . . .'   Proverbs 15:32

'It is much better to be criticised
   honestly for your faults . . .'   Proverbs 27:5

Deceit

'Those whose path is honest . . .' Proverbs 10:9

'A corrupt person earns an
   illusory profit . . .' Proverbs 11:18

'What is gained dishonestly may
   taste sweet for a moment . . .' Proverbs 20:17

'A good name is preferable to
   wealth . . .' Proverbs 22:1

'An honest answer . . .' Proverbs 24:26

Despair

'Everything is utterly futile . . .' Ecclesiastes 1:2-4,
   8, 9, 13, 14

'Even the sweetest of songs is as
   vinegar poured on a wound . . .' Proverbs 25:20a

Drunkenness

'Wine makes a mockery of you . . .' Proverbs 20:1

'Those who lack self-control . . .' Proverbs 25:28

'Look not on the wine when
   it is red . . .' Proverbs 23:31-3, 35

Envy

'All human effort and striving . . .' Ecclesiastes 4:4

'A contented heart leads to
   health . . .' Proverbs 14:30

'Wrath is forbidding . . .' Proverbs 27:4

Flattery

'Whoever flatters their
    neighbour . . .'   Proverbs 29:5

'Whoever delivers a well-earned
    rebuke . . .'   Proverbs 28:23

Forgiveness

'Friendship prospers where people
    are willing to admit mistakes . . .'   Proverbs 17:22

'The human spirit can cope
    with illness . . .'   Proverbs 18:14

Friendship

'Many claim to be faithful . . .'   Proverbs 20:6

'A friend is a constantly
    loving companion . . .'   Proverbs 17:17a

'Some people are fair-weather
    friends . . .'   Proverbs 18:24

'Well intended are the wounds
    inflicted by a friend . . .'   Proverbs 27:6

Generosity

'If you are able to help
    someone . . .'   Proverbs 3:27, 28

'Some people give
    freely . . .'   Proverbs 11:24, 25, 17

'The generous-hearted are
    richly blessed . . .'   Proverbs 22:9

'Truly, those who make goodness
    and kindness their aim . . .'   Proverbs 21:21

Gossip

'The words of a gossip are like
    tasty titbits . . .'   Proverbs 18:8

'If you hear people running
    you down . . .'   Ecclesiastes 7:21, 22

'A gossip divulges secrets . . .'   Proverbs 11:13

'An insincere person stirs up
    discord . . .'   Proverbs 16:28

'Scandalmongers will air in public what's
    revealed to them in private . . .'   Proverbs 20:19

Greed

'If you eat honey, take only as much
    as is enough for you . . .'   Proverbs 25:16, 27

'We labour day after day to feed
    our earthly appetites . . .'   Ecclesiastes 6:7

Happiness

'Those who are miserable in attitude
    will be miserable in life . . .'   Proverbs 15:15

'Happy are those who find wisdom and
    acquire understanding . . .' Proverbs 3:13, 14, 18

Health

'That which is pleasing to the eye
    brings joy to the heart . . .'   Proverbs 15:30

'A sunny disposition is an
    excellent medicine . . .'   Proverbs 17:22

'The human spirit can cope
with illness . . .'   Proverbs 18:14

Hope

'You have a future . . .'   Proverbs 23:18

'Hope unfulfilled makes the
heart sick . . .'   Proverbs 13:12

Humility

'A proud heart leads to
destruction . . .'   Proverbs 18:12

'When pride rears its head . . .'   Proverbs 11:2

'Just as silver is refined in a crucible
and gold in a furnace . . .'   Proverbs 27:21

'If you have been so foolish as
to exalt yourself . . .'   Proverbs 30:32

Integrity

'Those who preserve their integrity
will protect their soul . . .'   Proverbs 28:18, 6

Justice

'The field of the poor delivers
bountiful produce . . .'   Proverbs 13:23

'The one who exploits the needy
offends his Maker . . .'   Proverbs 14:21

'To oppress the poor is to insult
the one who created all . . .'   Proverbs 14:31

'If you shut your ears to the cry
of the needy . . .'   Proverbs 21:13

'Speak out for those denied a
  voice of their own . . .'   Proverbs 31:8, 9

'For I have seen the tears of the
  oppressed . . .'   Ecclesiastes 4:1

'Those who sow injustice will
  reap disaster . . .'   Proverbs 22:8, 16

Laughter

'The laughter of fools is like the
  crackling of kindling . . .'   Ecclesiastes 7:6

'It is thoughtless to mock
  others . . .'   Proverbs 11:12

'Even when we laugh the heart
  can be sad . . .'   Proverbs 14:13

'There is a time to laugh . . .'   Ecclesiastes 3:4

'A merry heart makes for a
  cheerful countenance . . .'   Proverbs 15:13, 15

Laziness

'Consider the ant, you lazy
  thing . . .'   Proverbs 6:6, 9

'Beware of loving sleep too
  much . . .'   Proverbs 20:13

'I passed by the field of one
  who was lazy . . .'   Proverbs 24:30-4

'The idle fail to plough when
  they should do . . .'   Proverbs 20:4

'Sow your seed in the morning . . .' Ecclesiastes 11:6

Loneliness

'There was a man with no
family . . .'   Ecclesiastes 4:8

'Two are better than one . . .'   Ecclesiastes 4:9-12

Love

'Hatred stirs up strife . . .'   Proverbs 10:12

'A simple meal seasoned with
love . . .'   Proverbs 15:17

'Never let go of love and
faithfulness . . .'   Proverbs 3:3

Patience

'It is better to be patient in
spirit . . .'   Proverbs 16:32a

'Better to be patient than
powerful . . .'   Ecclesiastes 7:8

Peace

'Whoever overlooks
wrongdoing . . .'   Proverbs 10:10

Prejudice

'As a saying of the wise has it . . .'   Proverbs 24:23

'It is wrong to be prejudiced
towards some . . .'   Proverbs 28:21

Pride

'Someone who promises much but delivers nothing . . .'	Proverbs 25:14
'Pride goes before our undoing . . .'	Proverbs 16:18
'An individual's pride will lead to them falling flat on their face . . .'	Proverbs 29:23
'A supercilious attitude and a proud heart . . .'	Proverbs 21:4
'It is better humbly to take a seat among the poor . . .'	Proverbs 16:19
'Let someone else flatter you . . .'	Proverbs 27:2

Quarrelling

'Starting a quarrel is like springing a leak.'	Proverbs 17:14
'Avoid arguing with someone . . .'	Proverbs 3:30
'Fools are invariably swift to quarrel . . .'	Proverbs 20:3
'A fire short of wood soon dies . . .'	Proverbs 26:20, 21

Relationships

'Iron can be used to sharpen iron . . .'	Proverbs 27:17

Religion

'God is greater than any human being . . .'	Job 36:22, 23, 26
'God has made everything beautiful in its time . . .'	Ecclesiastes 3:11

'When in the presence of the
divine . . .'   Ecclesiastes 5:2, 7

Remorse

'Those who do wrong are haunted
by guilt . . .'   Proverbs 28:1

'Not a single person on earth is
perfect . . .'   Ecclesiastes 7:20

'Who can claim, "I have cleansed
my heart from evil" . . . ?'   Proverbs 20:9

'No one who conceals mistakes
will prosper . . .'   Proverbs 28:13

Rest

'Those who work their land
will have sufficient . . .'   Proverbs 12:11, 14

'Better to enjoy a handful with
some well-earned rest . . .'   Ecclesiastes 4:6

Revenge

'Never say, "I will do to others what
they have done to me . . ."'   Proverbs 24:29

'If an enemy is hungry . . .'   Proverbs 25:21, 22

Sensitivity

'Each heart discerns its own
bitterness . . .'   Proverbs 14:10

'What someone means and desires
in their heart . . .'   Proverbs 20:5

'To offer good advice appropriate
to the circumstances . . .'   Proverbs 25:11

'How special it is to offer a word
in season . . .'   Proverbs 15:23

Sorrow

'Sorrow eats away at the human
heart . . .'   Proverbs 25:20b

'The more we learn the more we
have cause to grieve . . .'   Ecclesiastes 1:18

Time

'There is a season for
everything . . .'   Ecclesiastes 3:1-8

'Those who are in too much of
a hurry miss the way.'   Proverbs 19:2

Truth

'A falsehood has a fleeting life . . .'   Proverbs 12:19

'Get hold of truth and never
sell it.'   Proverbs 23:23

'Do not lose your grip on truth
or love . . .'   Proverbs 3:3

Wealth

'Do not exhaust yourself in an
effort to get rich . . .'   Proverbs 23:4, 5

'The miser rushes to get rich . . .'   Proverbs 28:22

'The wealthy believe their riches
   to be like a fortified city . . .'   Proverbs 18:11

'But riches do not last for ever.'   Proverbs 27:24

'Those who love money will never
   be satisfied by money alone . . .'   Ecclesiastes 5:10

'Those who give to the poor . . .'   Proverbs 28:27

Wisdom

'Obtain wisdom; cultivate insight.'   Proverbs 4:5

'Fools clothe themselves with
   folly . . .'   Proverbs 14:18

'The secret of becoming wise
   can be summed up thus . . .'   Proverbs 4:7-9

'Sensible people gain
   knowledge . . .'   Proverbs 18:15, 13, 17

'Unless they are guided wisely . . .'   Proverbs 11:14

'Only a fool believes they are
   always right . . .'   Proverbs 12:15

'If you are prepared to take
   advice and learn from it . . .'   Proverbs 19:20

'When I applied myself to
   acquiring wisdom . . .'   Ecclesiastes 8:16, 17

'What I have concluded is
   this . . .'   Ecclesiastes 7:23, 24